The ROSÉ
Lover's Companion

A Collection of Recipes,
Quotes, and Advice for
Wine Lovers

CECE MONROE

Skyhorse Publishing

Skyhorse Publishing books may be purchased in bulk at special discounts for sales promotion, corporate gifts, fund-raising, or educational purposes. Special editions can also be created to specifications. For details, contact the Special Sales Department, Skyhorse Publishing, 307 West 36th Street, 11th Floor, New York, NY 10018 or info@skyhorsepublishing.com.

Skyhorse® and Skyhorse Publishing® are registered trademarks of Skyhorse Publishing, Inc.®, a Delaware corporation.

Visit our website at www.skyhorsepublishing.com.

10 9 8 7 6 5 4 3 2 1

Library of Congress Cataloging-in-Publication Data is available on file.

Text by Peggy Jones
Interior design by Summersdale Publishers Ltd.
Front cover photograph: iStock

Print ISBN: 978-1-5107-4261-1
Ebook ISBN: 978-1-5107-4262-8

Printed in China

CONTENTS

. . . .

I SAY, WHAT *IS* ROSÉ?

As with all types of wine, rosé is made from fermented grape juice, taken from a wide variety of grapes. This versatility means it can be produced in many different climates. Take traditional "Old World" European wines as well as young and innovative "New World" wines, for example.

Rosé's beautiful shades of pink come from the brief amount of time the grape juice comes in contact with the skin of the grape: a process known as *maceration*. In rosés, this is allowed to occur for one to three days. In contrast, red wine macerates for up to one hundred days and often white wine isn't allowed to at all. A happy (and delightfully pink) medium!

ROSÉ BACK IN THE DAY

People all the way back in 4100 BC Armenia were producing what we now know as rosé. Pressing the grapes by hand (and foot) meant that their "red" wine didn't macerate for very long, creating lightly pigmented wine.

Although the Ancient Romans and Greeks upped the pressing game, darker wines were considered harsh and unsophisticated until well into the Middle Ages.

The rosé craze suffered a setback after World War Two, when Portuguese wine, popular in the United States, oxidized in its containers. The image of rosé being sickly sweet wasn't shaken until the early 2000s, when celebrities popularized it as an unpretentious yet thoroughly delicious drink.

THE ROSÉ

Europe currently holds the largest share of rosé production and consumption, but the United States is hot on its heels. Rosé is an important influence on emerging wine producers, too: it composes around 60 percent of Tunisia and Uruguay's growing wine markets. It won't be long until the rest of the world catches on.

REVOLUTION

Rosé is a refreshing move away from the formal style of "Old World" wine. It doesn't mature well, so there's no shame in enjoying a bottle with last year on the label! Best of all, you don't have to be a connoisseur to enjoy a glass; whether it's with a summer barbecue or simply sipping by the fire, rosé can be enjoyed in so many ways.

FIFTY
SHADES OF
pink

Generally, the lighter the color, the drier the wine will taste: rosés from Provence are the best known of this variety. Nearing the more vividly pink end of the spectrum, you will find sweeter and more fruity flavors; if this appeals to your palate, look out for white Zinfandels and delicate hues of the blushes. As well as still, rosé can be made semi- and fully-sparkling: rosé champagne is a highly sought-after variety. Depending on the region and producer, expect a range of notes from berries to citrus and watermelon.

WHAT YOU'LL NEED

You will be able to make most recipes in this book with standard kitchen equipment. However, if you want to be more adventurous, you might find the following equipment handy:

Glasses: All drink recipes will work in standard-sized tumblers and wine glasses. However, rocks, champagne, lowball, and Martini glasses can all enhance presentation!

Fun cookie cutters: These can be used to shape fruits for garnishing a drink in an especially decorative manner.

Cocktail shaker: This can be used to mix cocktails. To use one, place ice into your shaker with the ingredients and tighten the lid before shaking vigorously. When the shaker becomes ice cold, you know that the cocktail is ready to be decanted into a glass for serving.

Ice cream maker: Plenty of alternative ice cream making methods are available online, but an ice cream maker eases the process.

Mini molds: Affordable, and perfect for creating small ice cubes and gummy sweets!

GOOD COMPANY, GOOD WINE, GOOD WELCOME, CAN MAKE GOOD PEOPLE.

WILLIAM SHAKESPEARE

Stop and smell the rosé

SOBRIETY DIMINISHES,
DISCRIMINATES, AND
SAYS NO; DRUNKENNESS
EXPANDS, UNITES
AND SAYS YES.

WILLIAM JAMES

ROSÉ SPRITZER

(SERVES 1)

A spritzer is a delicious and refreshing drink, perfect for summer evenings or long lunches with friends.

INGREDIENTS

- 2 strawberries, halved
- 1 slice of lemon
- ½ fl. oz. (15 ml) sugar syrup
- 3 fl. oz. (85 ml) rosé
- Sparkling water
- Ice cubes
- Mint sprig and strawberry to garnish

METHOD

Gently muddle (lightly bruise with the back of a spoon) the strawberries and lemon in a tumbler to release the juices.

Add syrup and rosé, then fill the glass with ice and top with sparkling water.

Garnish with strawberry and mint sprigs and serve.

ROSÉ IS A WINE THAT ENTERTAINS LONG BEFORE IT EVEN PASSES YOUR LIPS.

MARK OLDMAN

PENICILLIN CURES, BUT WINE MAKES PEOPLE HAPPY.

ALEXANDER FLEMING

LONG, TALL, CHILLED-OUT ROSÉ

(SERVES 1)

Here is a fruity rosé twist on a classic tall cocktail recipe—stylish, yet so simple to make.

INGREDIENTS

- Ice cubes
- 3½ fl. oz. (100 ml) rich, fruity rosé
- ⅔ fl. oz. (20 ml) raspberry flavored vodka
- 1¼ fl. oz. (40 ml) fresh pink grapefruit juice
- Cherry soda, chilled
- Maraschino cherry to garnish

METHOD

Take a tall tumbler and half fill it with ice.

Pour in the wine, vodka, and juice. Stir gently before topping with your favorite cherry soda. It's quite sweet so add however much suits your taste.

Decorate with a maraschino cherry.

FOR WHEN

THE WINE IS IN,

THE WIT IS OUT.

THOMAS BECON

A MEAL WITHOUT WINE IS
LIKE A DAY WITHOUT
SUNSHINE.

JEAN ANTHELME BRILLAT-SAVARIN

MAY YOUR
WINE GLASS

never be

empty

SPICY PRAWN TAPAS

(SERVES 3)

Tapas, a traditional element of Spanish cuisine, is not any one particular kind of food—as long as it's served with a drink, anything served in a small appetiser-sized portion can be tapas.

INGREDIENTS

- 2 tbsp olive oil
- 2 garlic cloves, chopped
- 1 chilli, deseeded and chopped
- 150 g prawns, cooked and peeled
- 2 fl. oz. (60 ml) rosé
- Pinch salt
- Fresh parsley

METHOD

Heat the oil in a frying pan then add the garlic, chilli, and prawns and fry for a few minutes.

Add the rosé, salt, and parsley and simmer for another 5 minutes until the prawns are cooked through.

THE WORLD LOOKS BETTER THROUGH ROSÉ-TINTED GLASSES

EAT YOUR FOOD WITH GLADNESS, AND DRINK YOUR WINE WITH A JOYFUL HEART.

ECCLESIASTES 9:7

A GOOD ROSÉ...
IS A WINE
WHERE ONCE YOU
HAVE A GLASS
YOU SAY TO
YOURSELF, "WHY
NOT ANOTHER?"

ALAIN COMBARD

FROSÉ

· · · · · · · · · · ·

(SERVES 4–5)

This frozen drink is the classiest way to enjoy a slushie on a hot summer's day!

INGREDIENTS

- 75 g sugar
- 2 fl. oz. (60 ml) water
- Zest and juice of 1 lemon
- 1 bottle rosé

METHOD

Boil the sugar, water, lemon zest, and lemon juice until the sugar dissolves before straining and setting aside to cool.

In a shallow baking dish, decant and freeze the rosé until almost solid (3 hours minimum).

With a fork, scrape and break apart the frozen rosé into small chunks. Stir in the syrup according to how sweet you'd like the frosé. Keep in the freezer until you're ready to serve.

THE BEST WINES ARE THE ONES WE DRINK WITH FRIENDS

GIVE ME BOOKS, FRENCH WINE, FRUIT, FINE WEATHER, AND A LITTLE MUSIC.

JOHN KEATS

BEER IS MADE BY MEN, WINE BY GOD.

MARTIN LUTHER

FLAMINGO GLOW

(SERVES 1)

The bright notes of the orange lift the sweet flavors of this elegant cocktail.

INGREDIENTS

- Ice cubes
- 3½ fl. oz. (100 ml) rosé
- 1¼ fl. oz. (40 ml) bourbon whisky
- ⅔ fl. oz. (20 ml) orange juice
- Orange wedge to garnish

METHOD

Fill a tumbler with ice.

Shake all the ingredients in an ice-filled cocktail shaker before straining into the tumbler. Serve with an orange wedge hooked over the rim of the glass.

WHAT I LIKE TO DRINK MOST IS WINE THAT BELONGS TO OTHERS.

DIOGENES

WINE
A LITTLE,
LAUGH
A LOT

ALWAYS CARRY A CORKSCREW AND THE WINE SHALL PROVIDE ITSELF.

BASIL BUNTING

ROSÉ-STRAWBERRY POPS

. . . .

(SERVES 6)

These classy rosé ice pops are perfect for a scorching afternoon.

INGREDIENTS

- 6¾ fl. oz. (200 ml) rosé
- 6¾ fl. oz. (200 ml) water
- ½ fl. oz. (15 ml) lemon juice
- ¼ fl. oz. (5 ml) sugar syrup
- 150 g strawberries
- Fresh mint leaves (optional)

METHOD

In a large jug, stir in the rosé, water, lemon juice, and syrup, then refrigerate until cool.

Cut the strawberries lengthways into ¼-inch-thick slices resembling heart shapes and set them aside.

Evenly share the strawberry slices and fresh mint leaves between six ice-pop molds. Then fill the molds with the rosé and freeze until solid.

Yes way, rosé

I BELIEVE IN PINK.

Audrey Hepburn

LET US CELEBRATE THE
OCCASION WITH WINE
AND SWEET WORDS.

PLAUTUS

SUMMERTIME PUNCH

· ·

(SERVES 10)

The word punch *was adapted from the Sanskrit word for five, as the original drink comprised five ingredients: sugar, lemon, water, alcohol, and spices.*

INGREDIENTS

- ¼ melon
- 1 small peach
- 1 small nectarine
- 2 bottles chilled dry rosé
- 6 tbsp sugar
- 150 g raspberries

METHOD

Skin and deseed the melon, pit the peach and nectarine, and then chop the fruits into manageable, bite-sized pieces.

Pour the wine and sugar into a large jug. Throw in the sliced fruit and raspberries before refrigerating for 2 hours.

WINE AND
CHEESE ARE AGELESS
COMPANIONS.

M. F. K. FISHER

I just
rescued
some wine—
it was
trapped in
a bottle

EITHER GIVE

ME MORE WINE OR

LEAVE ME ALONE.

RUMI

ROSÉ REDUCTION

(SERVES 2)

This reduction is an excellent accompaniment to chicken and vegetables.

INGREDIENTS

- 30 g butter
- 30 g flour
- 2¼ fl. oz. (70 ml) rosé
- 50 g honey
- 7-8 fresh sage leaves
- Salt and pepper to season

METHOD

Melt the butter and flour in a small saucepan, stirring to eliminate lumps. Incorporate the rosé before bringing to a boil, stirring constantly.

Stir the mixture as you add the honey, sage, and seasoning, then boil for around 5 minutes to achieve a thick, sauce-like consistency.

A LOAF OF BREAD,
A JUG OF WINE,
AND THOU.

OMAR KHAYYAM

I ENJOY LONG
ROMANTIC
WALKS

down the

wine aisle

I NEVER TASTE THE WINE
FIRST IN RESTAURANTS,
I JUST ASK THE WAITER
TO POUR.

NIGELLA LAWSON

ALL WINES SHOULD BE
TASTED; SOME SHOULD
ONLY BE SIPPED, BUT
WITH OTHERS, DRINK
THE WHOLE BOTTLE.

PAULO COELHO

FROSÉ YOGURT

(SERVES 3)

A refreshing rosé twist on frozen yogurt.

INGREDIENTS

- 500 g plain Greek yogurt
- 150 g sugar
- ¼ tsp salt
- 4¼ fl. oz. (125 ml) dry rosé
- 2 fl. oz. (60 ml) pomegranate juice
- 2 tbsp fresh lemon juice
- 1 tbsp pomegranate molasses

METHOD

Whisk the yogurt, sugar, and salt in a freezer-safe bowl until the sugar has dissolved. Add the remaining ingredients.

Cover and allow the mixture to chill for 24 hours in the fridge. Transfer to a freezer for 2 hours before removing and beating with a fork.

Cover and place back in the freezer for 2 more hours to freeze until firm.

WINE IMPROVES WITH AGE;

I improve with wine

GIVE ME A BOWL OF WINE; IN THIS I BURY ALL UNKINDNESS.

WILLIAM SHAKESPEARE

FAN THE SINKING
FLAME OF HILARITY
WITH THE WING OF
FRIENDSHIP; AND PASS
THE ROSY WINE.

CHARLES DICKENS

ROSÉ WITH SUNSET FRUIT CUBES

· ·

(MAKES APPROX. 12 ICE CUBES)

These fruity ice cubes are the best way to keep your drink chilled without watering it down.

INGREDIENTS

- 1 fresh peach
- 4 fl. oz. (120 ml) water
- 150 g fresh raspberries
- 1 bottle rosé, chilled

METHOD

Pit and chop the peach then blitz in a food processor with half the water to a smooth purée. Use this to half fill the wells of an ice-cube tray.

Next, blitz the raspberries and remaining water until smooth. Use this to fully fill the ice-cube tray, then swirl the two layers together using a fork.

Freeze for 3 to 4 hours.

Add a couple of cubes to a wine glass and top with rosé to serve.

TO TAKE WINE
INTO OUR MOUTHS
IS TO SAVOUR A
DROPLET OF THE
RIVER OF HUMAN
HISTORY.

CLIFTON FADIMAN

THERE'S SOMETHING KIND OF DECADENT ABOUT DRINKING ROSÉ.

SAM DALY

TO "DRINK RESPONSIBLY" MEANS NOT TO SPILL IT

ROSÉ GRANITA WITH BLACKBERRIES

(SERVES 1)

Granita is similar to sorbet, but with a crunchier, more crystalline texture. Try experimenting with different fruity flavors to find your favorite.

INGREDIENTS

- 30 g fresh blackberries
- 8½ fl. oz. (250 ml) rosé
- 3½ fl. oz. (100 ml) water
- 3 tbsp caster sugar

METHOD

Crush the blackberries in a bowl before adding the wine, water, and sugar. Stir together until the sugar has dissolved completely.

Partially freeze the mixture in a shallow baking dish (about 1½ hours), before scraping with a fork to break up the mixture. Return the tray to the freezer to set solid. Scrape and break up the granita once more before serving.

HIDE OUR IGNORANCE AS WE WILL, AN EVENING OF WINE SOON REVEALS IT.

HERACLITUS

Where
there's
a will,
there's
a rosé

NOW

DROWN CARE IN WINE.

HORACE

STRAWBERRIES IN ROSÉ SYRUP

....

(SERVES 2–3)

This decadent dessert is both rich and refreshing, and sure to go down well at any party!

INGREDIENTS

- 1½ fl. oz. (45 ml) rosé
- 45 g icing sugar, divided
- 150 g strawberries
- 1 tsp crème de cassis
- ¼ tsp vanilla extract
- 5 fl. oz. (150 ml) heavy double cream
- 2 fresh basil leaves

METHOD

Put the wine in a bowl and add half the sugar. Stir this until the sugar is dissolved.

Hull and cut the strawberries lengthways, then coat them in the syrup and set aside.

Mix the crème de cassis, vanilla, and remaining sugar with the cream and beat until fluffy.

Top the strawberries with the cream and serve in small bowls. Decorate by topping with torn basil.

IT HAS BECOME QUITE A
COMMON PROVERB THAT
IN WINE THERE IS TRUTH.

PLINY THE ELDER

FROM WINE

WHAT SUDDEN
FRIENDSHIP SPRINGS!

JOHN GAY

ROSÉ SORBET

(SERVES 3–4)

The origin of sorbet is hotly contested, although European folklore tells that it originated with the Romans, who gathered snow from the Appian Way, brought it to Rome, and served it mixed with honey and wine.

INGREDIENTS

- 17 fl. oz. (500 ml) dry rosé
- 140 g granulated sugar
- 360 g raspberries, fresh or frozen
- Additional rosé for serving (optional)

METHOD

Boil the wine and sugar in a saucepan until the sugar has dissolved. Take off the heat, stir in the raspberries, and leave to cool. In a blender, purée the mixture before passing it through a sieve to remove the seeds. Then cover and refrigerate overnight.

Freeze the mixture for 2 hours, then remove and beat with a fork to break up ice crystals that are beginning to form. Cover and place back in the freezer for 2 more hours to freeze until firm.

ONE OF THE
DISADVANTAGES
OF WINE IS THAT
IT MAKES A MAN
MISTAKE WORDS
FOR THOUGHTS.

SAMUEL JOHNSON

WHAT CONTEMPTIBLE SCOUNDREL STOLE THE CORK FROM MY LUNCH?

W. C. Fields

WINE IS
BOTTLED
POETRY.

ROBERT LOUIS STEVENSON

BLACKBERRY BELLINI

. . . .

(SERVES 1)

Allegedly this cocktail is named after the artist Giovanni Bellini, who used a pale pink color in his work, similar to the shade of the drink. Traditionally Bellinis use Prosecco, but our rosé twist ensures that the cocktail retains its peachy blush.

INGREDIENTS

- 30 g blackberries
- Ice cubes
- ⅓ fl. oz. (10 ml) plain vodka
- 10 ml lemon juice
- 1 tsp caster sugar
- 3½ fl. oz. (100 ml) sparkling rosé, chilled

METHOD

Muddle (lightly bruise with the back of a spoon) the blackberries in a cocktail shaker. Add ice, vodka, lemon juice, and sugar.

Shake until cool and strain into a champagne glass. Top this up with rosé and serve.

SEIZE THE DAY!

then sip

rosé

WHAT'S DRINKING? A MERE PAUSE FROM THINKING!

LORD BYRON

ROSÉ GLAZE

(MAKES APPROX. 2 CUPS)

This glaze is delicious on ice cream and will keep well in an airtight container in the fridge.

INGREDIENTS

- 17 fl. oz. (500 ml) dry rosé
- 120 g sugar
- Zest of ½ a lemon
- 1 vanilla pod (seeds scraped out)
- 9¼ fl. oz. (275 ml) water
- 2 tsp freshly squeezed lemon juice

METHOD

In a pan over a high heat, simmer the wine, sugar, lemon zest, vanilla pod, and water until reduced to around three quarters of its original volume. This will take around 20 minutes.

Pass the syrup through a sieve, discarding the zest and pod.

Once the syrup has cooled to room temperature, add and stir in the lemon juice. Refrigerate until you're ready to serve.

SPARKLING AND BRIGHT,
IN LIQUID LIGHT,
DOES THE WINE OUR
GOBLETS GLEAM IN.

CHARLES FENNO HOFFMAN

AND WINE CAN OF THEIR
WITS THE WISE BEGUILE,
MAKE THE SAGE FROLIC,
AND THE SERIOUS SMILE.

HOMER

WINE CAN BE CONSIDERED
WITH GOOD REASON AS
THE MOST HEALTHFUL AND
THE MOST HYGIENIC OF
ALL BEVERAGES.

LOUIS PASTEUR

TIPSY STRAWBERRIES

. . . .

(SERVES 3–4)

Serve these over ice cream or as an elegant after-dinner treat.

INGREDIENTS

- 225 g strawberries, washed and hulled
- 5 fl. oz. (150 ml) rosé
- 1 fl. oz. (30 ml) vodka
- 25 g caster sugar

METHOD

Place the strawberries in a bowl and douse with the wine and vodka. Leave to chill in the fridge for at least 1 hour.

Drain the strawberries in a sieve or colander, then remove excess liquid with a paper towel.

Coat each strawberry in sugar before stowing them in the freezer until you're ready to enjoy.

I HAVE TAKEN MORE
OUT OF ALCOHOL THAN
ALCOHOL HAS TAKEN
OUT OF ME.

WINSTON CHURCHILL

I DRINK WHEN I HAVE OCCASION, AND SOMETIMES WHEN I HAVE NO OCCASION.

MIGUEL DE CERVANTES

YOU MAY
NOT BE
EVERYONE'S
CUP OF TEA,
BUT YOU'RE
SOMEONE'S
GLASS OF
WINE

CALIFORNIAN SUNSET

· ·

(SERVES 1)

The pomegranate molasses gives this bright and refreshing drink a richer depth of flavor.

INGREDIENTS

- 3½ fl. oz. (100 ml) rosé
- 2½ fl. oz. (75 ml) pomegranate molasses
- Juice from ½ a fresh orange
- Ice cubes
- Mango sorbet, to serve

METHOD

Pour the wine, molasses, and orange juice into a tumbler half full of ice cubes. Spoon in some mango sorbet, stir gently, and serve.

WINE
REPRESENTS
TO ME SHARING
AND GOOD
TIMES AND A
CELEBRATION
OF LIFE.

SAVE WATER—
drink rosé

ALCOHOL

MAY BE MAN'S WORST ENEMY, BUT THE BIBLE SAYS LOVE YOUR ENEMY.

FRANK SINATRA

ROSÉ RASPBERRY SORBET SECRETS

(SERVES 4–5)

Here's a creative way to serve your rosé—as well as keeping your drink deliciously cool!

INGREDIENTS

- 1 bottle sparkling rosé
- 17 fl. oz. (500 ml) raspberry sorbet
- Fresh mint to garnish

METHOD

For each drink, take a champagne flute and scoop in a small amount of sorbet.

Top this with sparkling rosé and garnish with mint. No hanging around—best drunk immediately!

JUST THE SIMPLE
ACT OF TASTING A
GLASS OF WINE IS
ITS OWN EVENT.

DAVID HYDE PIERCE

WINE IS SUNLIGHT, HELD TOGETHER BY WATER.

GALILEO

WINE, TAKEN IN
MODERATION, MAKES LIFE,
FOR A MOMENT, BETTER,
AND WHEN THE MOMENT
PASSES LIFE DOES NOT
FOR THAT REASON
BECOME WORSE.

BERNARD LEVIN

KIR AU VIN DE ROSÉ

· · · · · · · · · · · · · · · · · · ·

(SERVES 1)

There are a number of variations of this classic French cocktail of white wine and cassis: Kir Breton, made with Breton cider instead of wine; Kir Impérial, made with raspberry liqueur instead of cassis; and Kir Royal with champagne instead of wine. Here's our rosé variation!

INGREDIENTS

- 4¼ fl. oz. (125 ml) chilled rosé
- ¾ fl. oz. (25 ml) crème de cassis

METHOD

Take a wine glass and pour the cassis into the base. Simply top with rosé!

I SHALL DRINK NO WINE BEFORE IT'S TIME! OK, IT'S TIME.

GROUCHO MARX

WINE MAKES

DAILY LIVING EASIER,
LESS HURRIED, WITH FEWER
TENSIONS AND MORE
TOLERANCE.

BENJAMIN FRANKLIN

ROSÉ,
THEN
SLAY

ROSÉ AND PINK PEPPERCORN SAUCE

. . . .

(SERVES 2)

This sauce is perfect drizzled over cold meats and salad.

INGREDIENTS

- 8½ fl. oz. (250 ml)
- 2 tbsp balsamic vinegar
- 1 tbsp shallot, finely chopped
- ½ tsp salt
- 1 tsp pink peppercorns
- 2 sprigs fresh thyme
- 1 tbsp crème fraîche
- 125 g unsalted butter, chilled and cubed

METHOD

In a saucepan, gradually bring the first five ingredients to a boil. Turn the heat low once the liquid has reduced to 2 teaspoons (about 5 to 10 minutes).

Whisk in the crème fraîche, then take the pan off the heat and stir in the butter. Season with salt before pouring through a sieve; then serve.

OF ALL THINGS KNOWN
TO MORTALS, WINE IS THE
MOST POWERFUL AND
EFFECTUAL FOR EXCITING
AND INFLAMING THE
PASSIONS OF MANKIND.

FRANCIS BACON

START A JUICE CLEANSE.

GRAPE JUICE.

FERMENTED.

WINE.

BE CAREFUL
TO TRUST A PERSON
WHO DOES NOT
LIKE WINE.

KARL MARX

LAMB IN ROSÉ

· ·

(SERVES 2)

This warming and luxurious recipe is ideal for romantic date nights or cozy evenings with friends.

INGREDIENTS

- 3 tbsp vegetable oil
- 250 g boneless lamb, cubed
- 1 small onion, diced
- 1 red pepper, seeded and cut into chunks
- 2 carrots, sliced

- 4 fl. oz. (120 ml) vegetable stock
- 2½ fl. oz. (75 ml) rosé
- Handful fresh rosemary leaves
- ½ tbsp corn starch blended with 1 tbsp water

METHOD

Heat oil in a large saucepan on a medium-high heat. Add the lamb and cook for 10 minutes, stirring occasionally, until golden brown.

Add the onion, pepper, and carrots and cook for 3 minutes. Stir in the remaining ingredients. Bring to a boil then reduce heat to low and simmer for 20 minutes until the lamb is tender. Season to taste.

A MAN WILL BE ELOQUENT IF YOU GIVE HIM GOOD WINE.

Ralph Waldo Emerson

ONE NOT ONLY

DRINKS WINE, ONE SMELLS IT,
OBSERVES IT, TASTES IT, SIPS IT,
AND—ONE TALKS ABOUT IT.

KING EDWARD VII

EVERY BOX OF RAISINS IS A TRAGIC TALE OF GRAPES THAT COULD HAVE BEEN WINE

ROSÉ RISOTTO WITH THYME

(SERVES 2–3)

This creamy risotto recipe is a perfect weeknight treat, and so simple to put together.

INGREDIENTS

- 2 tbsp olive oil
- 1 small onion
- 350 g risotto rice
- 4¼ fl. oz. (125 ml) rosé
- 1 quart chicken stock
- 2 tsp salt
- 1 tsp black pepper
- 3 sprigs thyme
- 100 g Parmesan

METHOD

Heat oil in a large saucepan over a medium heat. Add onion (chopped) and fry until softened (2 to 3 minutes). Add rice and stir well.

Pour in the wine and allow to bubble for 30 seconds. Then add stock, salt, pepper, and thyme. Bring to the boil then simmer uncovered for 10 minutes, stirring frequently, until the rice is almost tender and the risotto looks creamy. Then stir in the cheese and cook for a further 5 minutes. The rice should be tender with a slight bite.

Working
nine
to wine

WINES ARE WONDERS; GREAT WINES ARE MAGICAL.

William E. Massee

GOD MADE
ONLY WATER, BUT
MAN MADE WINE.

VICTOR HUGO

ROSE-PERFUMED ROSÉ

. . . .

(SERVES 6)

With its floral scent and rose-sugar garnish, there's surely no prettier way to sip your rosé.

INGREDIENTS

- 115 g sugar
- 1½ tsp dried roses
- 1 bottle rosé, lightly chilled
- About 6 splashes of rose water

METHOD

Blitz the sugar and rose petals in a processor to create an evenly textured powder, then place on a plate.

Run a wet finger around the rim of six wine glasses and dip them into the rose sugar.

Divide the wine equally between the glasses: use a funnel to avoid ruining the sugar rim. Next add a small splash of rose water to each glass before serving.

WINE CAN BE A BETTER
TEACHER THAN INK.

STEPHEN FRY

QUICKLY, BRING ME
A BEAKER OF WINE,
SO THAT I MAY WET
MY MIND AND SAY
SOMETHING CLEVER.

ARISTOPHANES

THE DISCOVERY
OF A GOOD WINE
IS INCREASINGLY
BETTER FOR
MANKIND THAN
THE DISCOVERY
OF A NEW STAR.

LEONARDO DA VINCI

ZESTY PINK GIMLET

. . . .

(SERVES 1)

The name of this cocktail allegedly derives from the tool of the same name, which is used for drilling small holes—the connection between the two being the cocktail's sharp and piercing flavor!

INGREDIENTS

- 2½ fl. oz (75 ml) rosé
- ¾ fl. oz. (25 ml) gin
- ¾ fl. oz. (25 ml) lime cordial
- Ice cubes
- Thin strip of lime zest

METHOD

Add the wine, gin, and cordial to a cocktail shaker filled with ice. Stir until cold before straining into a Martini glass.

Garnish with a twist of lime zest.

WINE: IT'S IN MY VEINS AND
I CAN'T GET IT OUT.

BURGESS MEREDITH

ROSÉ
THE DAY
AWAY

THERE MUST

BE ALWAYS WINE
AND FELLOWSHIP OR
WE ARE TRULY LOST.

ANN FAIRBAIRN

WARMED RUBY ROSÉ

· ·

(SERVES 4–5)

With warming spices and plenty of fruity flavors, this drink has a lot going on. It's the perfect accompaniment to cozy winter evenings.

INGREDIENTS

- 1 bottle rosé
- 5 cardamom pods
- 2 tsp stem ginger, sliced
- 1 cinnamon stick
- ¼ pink grapefruit, sliced
- 2 tbsp crème de cassis

METHOD

Fetch a big saucepan and pour in the wine, cardamom, stem ginger, cinnamon, and the grapefruit slices.

Simmer over a medium heat before adding the cassis and stirring.

Pour through a sieve into a jug and serve.

WINE IS THE SORT OF
BEVERAGE THAT DOES
NOT DESTROY BUT
ENRICHES LIFE.

BILL ST JOHN

ROSÉ IS THE ANSWER...

what was the question?

SIP,
SWIRL,
SWALLOW!

MICHELINE R. RAMOS

CHERRIES IN ROSÉ SYRUP

. . . .

(SERVES 4)

This fruity dessert is sure to be a winner at any gathering—whether it's an intimate evening for two or a large party with friends.

INGREDIENTS

- 13½ fl. oz. (400 ml) rosé
- 2 tbsp crème de cassis
- 1 vanilla pod
- 100 g caster sugar
- 500 g cherries

METHOD

Boil the wine, cassis, vanilla pod, and sugar in a pan until the sugar has dissolved.

Remove the stones from the cherries, then add the fruit to the pan and cook on a low heat for around 5 minutes. Remove the cherries and set them aside in a bowl. Turn up the heat up and reduce the syrup until thickened.

Serve the cherries in individual bowls with the syrup poured over the top. You can enjoy this warm or cold.

A BOTTLE OF WINE
BEGS TO BE SHARED;
I HAVE NEVER MET A
MISERLY WINE LOVER.

CLIFTON FADIMAN

Wine
flies when
you're
having
fun

DRINKING
WINE

IS JUST A PART
OF LIFE, LIKE
EATING FOOD.

FRANCIS FORD COPPOLA

BOOZY STRAWBERRY SYLLABUB

. . . .

(SERVES 6)

Syllabub is a dessert based on a traditional English drink of the same name. In the original drink, milk or cream was curdled with acid, such as wine or cider, and then sweetened.

INGREDIENTS

- 400 g strawberries, hulled and halved
- 4 tbsp caster sugar
- 4 tbsp rosé
- 5¾ fl. oz. (170 ml) heavy cream

METHOD

Place the strawberries, sugar, and wine in a dish to marinate for 30 minutes.

Remove the strawberries and spoon them evenly into four large wine glasses. Next, pour the cream into the bowl containing the leftover juice and whip into soft peaks before using it to top the fruit.

A GOOD WINE IS LIKE A
GENTLE KISS, ITS EFFECT
THROUGHOUT THE MEAL
IS SCINTILLATINGLY
SENSUAL IN AN ELEGANTLY
UNDERSTATED WAY.

FRANCES TABEEK

GOOD WINE PRAISES ITSELF.

Dutch proverb

NOROSÉPHOBIA: THE FEAR OF RUNNING OUT OF ROSÉ

SPICY ROAST RHUBARB WITH GINGER

(SERVES 6–8)

Add some heat to your rosé with this spicy dessert.

INGREDIENTS

- 700 g rhubarb
- 6 strips orange zest
- 2 star anises
- 2 tsp stem ginger
- Small glass rosé
- 85 g caster sugar
- 250 g mascarpone

METHOD

Preheat oven to 392°F (200°C). Slice the rhubarb into short batons and place into a shallow baking dish, spreading the zest, star anises, and ginger (sliced) evenly among it. Pour in the rosé and sprinkle dish with sugar.

Cover securely with foil and roast for 20 minutes. The rhubarb should be tender. Return dish to the oven for another 5 minutes, uncovered, until the sauce has reduced. Serve with a spoonful of mascarpone.

THERE IS SOMETHING
TERRIBLY COMPELLING
ABOUT ROSÉ ON A
SUMMER'S DAY.

JANCIS ROBINSON

Rosé, s'il vous plaît

WINE IS CONNECTED TO ABUNDANCE.

CAROLE BOUQUET

IF WE SIP THE WINE, WE
FIND DREAMS COMING
UPON US OUT OF THE
IMMINENT NIGHT.

D. H. LAWRENCE

THE ROSÉ BLUSH BOUQUET

(SERVES 1)

Enjoy the flavors of honey, citrus, and lavender with this sophisticated cocktail.

INGREDIENTS

- Ice cubes
- 2½ fl. oz. (75 ml) rosé
- 1¼ fl. oz. (38 ml) gin
- ¾ fl. oz. (21 ml) Lillet Blanc
- 2½ fl. oz. (75 ml) orange juice
- 1 lavender sprig

METHOD

Fill a lowball glass three quarters of the way with ice and add the rosé.

Pour the gin, Lillet Blanc, and orange juice over the top before serving with a sprig of lavender.

I DO LOVE MY WINE.
I'D OPT TO DRINK MY
CALORIES RATHER THAN
EAT THEM EVERY TIME.

RACHEL NICHOLS

GREAT WINE

IS ALWAYS ENHANCED
BY GREAT FOOD.

KENNETH CRANHAM

ROSÉ-STEAMED MUSSELS

. . . .

(SERVES 4)

Serve with crusty bread and a leafy side salad.

INGREDIENTS

- 2 tbsp olive oil
- 2 garlic cloves, crushed
- 2 shallots, finely chopped
- 8½ fl. oz. (250 ml) rosé
- 6 lbs (2.7 kg) mussels, scrubbed and debearded
- 3 tbsp unsalted butter
- Salt and pepper
- 2 tbsp chopped parsley

METHOD

Heat the oil in a large pot. Add garlic and shallots and cook on a low heat until translucent. Then add wine and bring to the boil. Add mussels, cover and cook, shaking the pot occasionally until all the mussels have opened (approx. 5 minutes).

Remove mussels and place them in individual bowls. Add butter to the sauce and season well. Pour this over the mussels, taking care to avoid any grit at the bottom of the pan. Serve sprinkled with the parsley.

WINE... IS THE
ONLY BEVERAGE
THAT FEEDS
THE BODY, SOUL,
AND SPIRIT OF
MAN AND AT
THE SAME TIME
STIMULATES
THE MIND.

ROBERT MONDAVI

THIS ROSÉ PAIRS PERFECTLY WITH

more of this rosé

ALCOHOL MAKES OTHER PEOPLE LESS TEDIOUS, AND FOOD LESS BLAND.

CHRISTOPHER HITCHENS

SUMMER FRUITS POACHED IN ROSÉ

(SERVES 6–8)

This dish is simple but striking and makes a wonderful light summer dessert.

INGREDIENTS

- 225 g sugar
- ½ vanilla bean, split
- 2 strips of lemon zest
- 21 fl. oz. (625 ml) dry rosé
- 4 ripe plums, pitted and halved
- 4 ripe apricots, pitted and halved
- 4 nectarines, pitted and quartered

METHOD

Place the sugar, vanilla, lemon zest, and rosé in a large pan and bring to the boil to dissolve the sugar. Add the plums, apricots, and nectarines. Cook on a medium heat until the fruit is tender, about 5 to 8 minutes.

Let the fruit and liquid cool before refrigerating until chilled. Place the fruit into separate dishes and spoon over the syrup.

DON'T CRY OVER SPILLED MILK: IT COULD HAVE BEEN ROSÉ

WINE SPEAKS TO ALL THE SENSES.

MARY LOU POSCH

IF REASSURANCES COULD
DULL PAIN, NOBODY WOULD
EVER GO TO THE TROUBLE
OF PRESSING GRAPES.

SCOTT LYNCH

CIDER WITH ROSIE
· ·

(SERVES 1)

This drink is a bold fusion of fruit flavors and perfect for those who enjoy their cocktails on the sweeter side.

INGREDENTS
- 1 tbsp caster sugar
- 1 tsp cinnamon
- 1 tbsp pomegranate molasses
- ⅔ fl. oz. (20 ml) orange juice
- 1 tbsp lemon juice
- 2½ fl. oz. (75 ml) rosé
- 1 tbsp Calvados

METHOD
Mix the sugar and cinnamon together on a small plate. Coat the rims of the glasses by dipping them into the pomegranate molasses, then into the cinnamon sugar.

Place the orange and lemon juice into a glass and top with rosé and Calvados.

IT WAS A FINE NIGHT, A WARM NIGHT, A WINE-DRINKING NIGHT.

JACK KEROUAC

SORROW CAN BE ALLEVIATED BY GOOD SLEEP, A BATH, AND A GLASS OF WINE.

Thomas Aquinas

THE MORE ROSÉ I DRINK, THE BETTER I GET AT PRONOUNCING ITS NAME

SANGRIA ROSA

. . . .

(SERVES 1)

Sangria is traditional to Spain, although early recipes have also been traced back to Portugal, Ireland, and Greece. We've added rosé to this classic recipe of fruit, brandy, and orange juice.

INGREDIENTS

- Ice cubes
- 3½ fl. oz. (100 ml) rosé
- 1¾ fl. oz. (50 ml) fresh orange juice
- ⅓ fl. oz. (10 ml) brandy
- ⅓ fl. oz. (10 ml) Cointreau
- 2½ fl. oz. (75 ml) lemonade
- Fresh orange and lemon slices to garnish

METHOD

Place a few ice cubes into a tall glass then pour in all the ingredients, making sure to add the lemonade last.

Gently stir ingredients together and decorate with the fruit slices.

EVERYTHING'S BETTER
WITH SOME WINE
IN THE BELLY.

GEORGE R. R. MARTIN

WINE MEANS THE RESPONSIBLE PART OF THE DAY IS OVER.

JULIE JAMES

DRUNKEN PINK LEMONADE

· ·

(SERVES 3–4)

The New York Times *obituary for Henry E. Allott (d. 1912) claims Allott made the original glass of pink lemonade when he dropped some red cinnamon sweets into his glass by accident (although this is subject to some debate).*

INGREDIENTS

- 2 fl. oz. (60 ml) water
- 55 g sugar
- 2 fl. oz. (60 ml) fresh lemon juice
- 8½ fl. oz. (250 ml) cold water
- 8½ fl. oz. (250 ml) rosé

METHOD

Add the water and sugar to a small pan. Boil to dissolve the sugar before leaving to cool.

Pour the lemon juice and cold water into the syrup, stirring to dissolve. Put in the fridge until cold.

To serve, mix your homemade lemonade with the rosé.

WINE GIVES ONE "IDEAS."

Roman Payne

WINE MAKES EVERY MEAL AN OCCASION, EVERY TABLE MORE ELEGANT, EVERY DAY MORE CIVILIZED.

ANDRE SIMON

FRUITY ROSÉ JELLIES

· ·

(MAKES APPROX. 12)

Why not try experimenting with different fruits for this simple yet tasty dessert?

INGREDIENTS

- 8½ fl. oz. (250 ml) rosé
- 115 g sugar
- 3 tsp gelatine powder
- 150 g mixture of blueberries, raspberries, and diced strawberries

METHOD

Place the wine in a microwave-safe container and heat for 2 minutes. Stir in the sugar and gelatine and whisk until completely dissolved, then allow to cool.

Divide the fruit evenly into ice-cube trays then top up with the liquid and allow to set. Keep in the fridge for at least 1 hour before serving.

WE ARE ALL MORTAL UNTIL
THE FIRST KISS AND THE
SECOND GLASS OF WINE.

EDUARDO GALEANO

EVERYBODY'S GOT TO BELIEVE IN SOMETHING. I BELIEVE I'LL HAVE ANOTHER DRINK.

PETER DE VRIES

NOW IS THE TIME FOR DRINKING, NOW THE TIME TO DANCE FOOTLOOSE UPON THE EARTH.

Horace

I'd rather be drinking rosé

LIFE ISN'T ALL DIAMONDS AND ROSÉ, BUT IT SHOULD BE.

LISA VANDERPUMP

IMAGE CREDITS

Corkscrew on pp.30, 71, 87, 139 – © Twin Design/Shutterstock.com

Bottle and corkscrew outline on pp.42, 59, 119 – © Luci Ward

Bottle and glass engraving on pp.5, 7, 35, 39, 48, 63, 66, 76, 88, 94, 114, 122, 140, 153, 157, 160 – © Nata Alhontess/Shutterstock.com

Bottle and glass silhouette on pp.18, 55, 90 – © nikolae/Shutterstock.com

Bubbles on pp.22, 47, 74, 106, 110, 126, 147 – © Oxy_gen/Shutterstock.com

Grapes engraving on pp.19, 33, 45, 59, 75, 86, 107, 119, 131, 148 – © BrSav/Shutterstock.com

Large glass shape on pp.3, 27, 54, 82, 108, 134, 154 – © natrot/Shutterstock.com

Large grapes silhouette on pp.34, 62, 72, 92, 111, 147 – © Best Vector Elements/Shutterstock.com

Pouring bottle silhouette on pp.17, 20, 24, 28, 32, 36, 40, 44, 49, 53, 57, 61, 65, 69, 73, 77, 81, 85, 89, 93, 97, 101, 105, 109, 113, 117, 121, 125, 130, 133, 137, 141, 145, 149, 152 – © Luci Ward

Small grapes icon on pp.16, 31, 41, 52, 68, 80, 96, 104, 116, 129, 144, 151 – © Ivan Negin/Shutterstock.com

Wine glass silhouette on pp.14, 26, 51, 79, 128 – © zizi_mentos/Shutterstock.com

Wine ring on pp.15, 37, 102, 127, 156 – © Anna Kutukova/Shutterstock.com

Wine glass sketch on p.1 – © zizi_mentos/Shutterstock.com